C000057768

# CHOOSE HAPPY

summersdale

CHOOSE HAPPY

An Hachette UK Company
www.hachette.co.uk

Summersdale Publishers Ltd
Part of Octopus Publishing Group Limited
Carmelite House
50 Victoria Embankment
LONDON
EC4Y 0DZ
UK

www.summersdale.com

Printed and bound in the Czech Republic

ISBN: 978-1-78685-561-9

Substantial discounts on bulk quantities of Summersdale books are available to corporations, professional associations and other organisations. For details contact general enquiries: telephone: +44 (0) 1243 771107 or email: enquiries@summersdale.com.

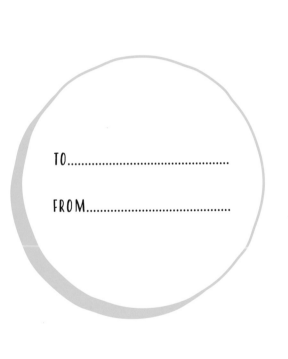

TO.........................................

FROM.......................................

SOMETIMES THE SMALLEST
STEP IN THE RIGHT DIRECTION
ENDS UP BEING THE BIGGEST
STEP OF YOUR LIFE.

EMMA STONE

I DON'T THINK THAT
THERE ARE ANY
LIMITS TO HOW

*excellent*

WE COULD MAKE
LIFE SEEM.

JONATHAN SAFRAN FOER

EVEN IF EVERY
DAY ISN'T
HAPPY, THERE'S
HAPPINESS IN
EVERY DAY

JOY COMES NOT
THROUGH POSSESSION
OR OWNERSHIP,
BUT THROUGH
A WISE AND
LOVING HEART.

BUDDHIST PROVERB

# ACT THE WAY
# YOU WANT TO FEEL.

GRETCHEN RUBIN

You should put
a good deal of
thought into the
— happiness —
that you are
able to give.

ELEANOR ROOSEVELT

# RADIATE
# JOY

MOST PEOPLE ARE
AS HAPPY AS THEY
MAKE THEIR

*minds*

UP TO BE.

ANONYMOUS

*Those who bring*

*— sunshine —*

*into the lives
of others cannot
keep it from
themselves.*

J. M. BARRIE

HAPPINESS CAN
BE TWO THINGS:
**A FEELING**
WE NOTICE,
AND A CHOICE
WE MAKE

IT'S WHAT'S
IN YOURSELF THAT
MAKES YOU HAPPY
OR UNHAPPY.

AGATHA CHRISTIE

IF YOU WANT
OTHERS TO BE HAPPY,
PRACTISE COMPASSION.
IF YOU WANT TO BE HAPPY,
PRACTISE COMPASSION.

DALAI LAMA

*Happiness is not the*

*— absence —*

*of problems;*
*it's the ability to*
*deal with them.*

STEVE MARABOLI

# COLLECT
# MOMENTS,
# NOT
# THINGS

IT'S NOT SELFISH
TO LOVE YOURSELF,
TAKE CARE OF YOURSELF,
AND TO MAKE
HAPPINESS A PRIORITY.
IT'S A NECESSITY.

MANDY HALE

HAPPINESS
QUITE UNSHARED
CAN SCARCELY BE
CALLED HAPPINESS;
IT HAS NO TASTE.

CHARLOTTE BRONTË

RIGHT NOW IS
THE BEST TIME
TO BE HAPPY

THERE IS NO WAY
TO HAPPINESS –
HAPPINESS IS
THE WAY.

THÍCH NHẤT HẠNH

JOY IS WHAT HAPPENS
TO US WHEN WE ALLOW
OURSELVES TO RECOGNISE
HOW GOOD THINGS
REALLY ARE.

MARIANNE WILLIAMSON

The art of
being happy lies in
the power of extracting
happiness from
common things.

**Henry Ward Beecher**

LOOK ON THE

# BRIGHT

SIDE

HAPPINESS CAN BE THOUGHT,
TAUGHT AND CAUGHT...
BUT NOT BOUGHT.

HARVEY MACKAY

DON'T HURRY,
DON'T WORRY.
AND BE SURE
TO SMELL THE

*flowers*

ALONG
THE WAY.

WALTER HAGEN

# DON'T LET A BAD FIVE MINUTES SPOIL A WHOLE GOOD DAY

*Knowledge*
*of what is*
*— possible —*
*is the beginning*
*of happiness.*

GEORGE SANTAYANA

SEEK TO DO GOOD
AND YOU WILL FIND
THAT HAPPINESS WILL
RUN AFTER YOU.

JAMES FREEMAN CLARKE

IF YOU
WANT TO BE
HAPPY, BE.

LEO TOLSTOY

WE CAN'T
ALTER THE WIND,
BUT WE CAN
ANGLE THE SAILS

LOVE ONE ANOTHER
AND YOU WILL BE HAPPY.
IT'S AS SIMPLE AND AS
DIFFICULT AS THAT.

MICHAEL LEUNIG

HAPPINESS IS
NOT A MATTER
OF EVENTS;
IT DEPENDS
UPON THE

*tides*

OF THE MIND.

ALICE MEYNELL

DON'T PUT THE
KEY TO YOUR
JOY IN THE
POCKET OF
SOMEONE ELSE

THE HAPPIEST PEOPLE
SEEM TO BE THOSE
WHO HAVE NO PARTICULAR
CAUSE FOR BEING
HAPPY EXCEPT THAT
THEY ARE SO.

WILLIAM RALPH INGE

HAPPINESS IS
A WELL-BALANCED
COMBINATION OF LOVE,
LABOUR AND LUCK.

MARY WILSON LITTLE

Resolve to keep happy,

and your joy and you

shall form an

— invincible host —

against difficulties.

HELEN KELLER

FIND
SOMETHING
POSITIVE IN
EACH DAY

A HEART
FULL OF

*joy*

IS BETTER
THAN A HANDFUL
OF COINS.

MATSHONA DHLIWAYO

Happiness is
an occasional brief
glance into how
— simple —

it all can be.

ROBERT BRAULT

DO WHAT
MAKES YOU HAPPY,
WITH SOMEONE
WHO MAKES YOU
**SMILE**

LAUGHING MAKES
EVERYTHING EASIER.

CARMEN ELECTRA

WITHOUT A HUMBLE BUT
REASONABLE CONFIDENCE
IN YOUR OWN POWERS,
YOU CANNOT BE
SUCCESSFUL OR HAPPY.

NORMAN VINCENT PEALE

Happiness is the
best make-up;
— a smile —
is better than
any lipstick
you'll put on.

DREW BARRYMORE

# IF IT COSTS YOUR HAPPINESS, IT COSTS TOO MUCH

THE PROBLEM WITH PEOPLE
IS THEY FORGET THAT
MOST OF THE TIME
IT'S THE SMALL THINGS
THAT COUNT.

JENNIFER NIVEN

HAPPINESS
IS NOT BEING
PAINED IN BODY OR
TROUBLED IN MIND.

THOMAS JEFFERSON

PEOPLE WAIT
ALL WEEK
FOR FRIDAY,
ALL YEAR
FOR SUMMER,
ALL LIFE FOR
HAPPINESS

IF YOU ARE HAPPY,
YOU CAN GIVE
HAPPINESS.

GISELE BÜNDCHEN

THERE CAN BE NO
HAPPINESS IF THE THINGS
WE BELIEVE IN ARE
DIFFERENT FROM THE
THINGS WE DO.

FREYA STARK

It is more fitting for
a man to laugh at life
than to lament over it.

**Seneca**

TO REACH
HAPPINESS, YOU
MUST FIRST
**REACH**
FOR IT

IF YOU WANT TO BE HAPPY,
SET A GOAL THAT
COMMANDS YOUR THOUGHTS,
LIBERATES YOUR ENERGY AND
INSPIRES YOUR HOPES.

ANDREW CARNEGIE

WHAT A
WONDERFUL
LIFE I'VE HAD!
I ONLY WISH I'D

*realised*

IT SOONER.

COLETTE

BE HAPPY
WITH WHO
YOU ARE,
NOT WHO YOU
THINK YOU
SHOULD BE

*Happiness is*
*when what you*
*— think, —*
*what you*
*— say, —*
*and what you*
*— do —*
*are in harmony.*

MAHATMA GANDHI

THREE GRAND
ESSENTIALS
TO HAPPINESS
IN THIS LIFE ARE
SOMETHING TO DO,
SOMETHING TO LOVE,
AND SOMETHING
TO HOPE FOR.

JOSEPH ADDISON

THE HAPPINESS
OF YOUR LIFE DEPENDS
UPON THE QUALITY OF
YOUR THOUGHTS.

MARCUS AURELIUS

WHY COUNT
YOUR TROUBLES
WHEN YOU CAN
COUNT YOUR
BLESSINGS?

HAPPINESS IS A PERFUME
YOU CANNOT POUR
ON OTHERS WITHOUT
GETTING SOME
ON YOURSELF.

RALPH WALDO EMERSON

THE BEST
WAY TO CHEER
YOURSELF IS TO
TRY TO CHEER

*somebody*

*else*

UP.

MARK TWAIN

DON'T LET
SOME SILLY OLD
THING BRING
YOU DOWN

SOMETIMES YOUR JOY
IS THE SOURCE OF YOUR
SMILE, BUT SOMETIMES
YOUR SMILE CAN BE
THE SOURCE OF
YOUR JOY.

THÍCH NHẤT HẠNH

HAPPINESS
IS A HABIT -
CULTIVATE IT.

ELBERT HUBBARD

*I am convinced that life is 10 per cent what happens to me and 90 per cent — how I react — to it.*

CHARLES R. SWINDOLL

# TODAY, I CHOOSE HAPPY

NEVER GIVE UP,
BECAUSE YOU
NEVER KNOW
WHAT THE

*tide*

WILL BRING IN
THE NEXT DAY.

TOM HANKS

*Happiness depends*
*more on the*
*— inward disposition —*
*of mind than*
*on outward*
*circumstances.*

BENJAMIN FRANKLIN

LIVE ONE
**SMILE**
AT A TIME

THE SECRET
OF HAPPINESS
IS TO ADMIRE
WITHOUT
DESIRING.

CARL SANDBURG

WORRY NEVER
ROBS TOMORROW
OF ITS SORROW.
IT ONLY SAPS TODAY
OF ITS JOY.

LEO BUSCAGLIA

*Happiness is not something you postpone for the future; it is something you*

*— design —*

*for the present.*

JIM ROHN

# THERE ARE SO MANY WONDERFUL REASONS TO BE HAPPY

DON'T WASTE A
MINUTE NOT BEING HAPPY.
IF ONE WINDOW CLOSES,
RUN TO THE NEXT WINDOW,
OR BREAK DOWN A DOOR.

BROOKE SHIELDS

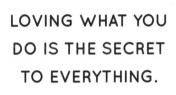

LOVING WHAT YOU
DO IS THE SECRET
TO EVERYTHING.

JULIA ROBERTS

LIVE WELL.
LAUGH LOUD.
SMILE OFTEN.

HAPPINESS IS
FOUND IN DOING,
NOT MERELY
POSSESSING.

NAPOLEON HILL

I'VE HAD TO LEARN
TO FIGHT ALL MY LIFE –
GOT TO LEARN TO
KEEP SMILING.
IF YOU SMILE,
THINGS WORK OUT.

SERENA WILLIAMS

If you're not happy,
you can become happy.
Happiness is a choice.

**Jennifer Aniston**

NEW WAYS TO
**THINK**
BREED NEW
WAYS TO BE

ENJOY YOUR OWN LIFE
WITHOUT COMPARING IT WITH
THAT OF ANOTHER.

MARQUIS DE CONDORCET

THE FIRST RECIPE
FOR HAPPINESS IS:
AVOID TOO LENGTHY

*meditation*

ON THE PAST.

ANDRÉ MAUROIS

# THINK
# HAPPY
# THOUGHTS

Optimism is a
happiness magnet.
If you
— stay positive —
good things and
good people will be
drawn to you.

MARY LOU RETTON

WE DON'T STOP PLAYING
BECAUSE WE GROW OLD;
WE GROW OLD BECAUSE
WE STOP PLAYING.

GEORGE BERNARD SHAW

HAPPINESS
DEPENDS UPON
OURSELVES.

ARISTOTLE

YOU KNOW
THOSE THINGS
YOU ALWAYS
SAID YOU
WANTED TO DO?
GO DO THEM.

A SMILE IS A
CURVE THAT SETS
EVERYTHING STRAIGHT.

PHYLLIS DILLER

IF YOU ARE
TOO BUSY TO
*laugh,*
YOU ARE
TOO BUSY.

PROVERB

IF IT
DOESN'T MAKE
YOU HAPPY,
PERHAPS IT ISN'T
WORTH IT

HAPPINESS IS SOMETHING
THAT COMES INTO OUR LIVES
THROUGH DOORS WE DON'T
EVEN REMEMBER
LEAVING OPEN.

ROSE WILDER LANE

THAT MAN IS
RICHEST WHOSE
PLEASURES ARE
CHEAPEST.

HENRY DAVID THOREAU

One of the simplest ways
to stay happy is by
— letting go —
of the things
that make
you sad.

ANONYMOUS

# LIVE IN THE MOMENT

THE SUMMIT
OF HAPPINESS
IS REACHED WHEN
A PERSON IS

*ready to be*

WHAT HE IS.

ERASMUS

The important thing
to you is not how many
years in your life, but
— how much life —
in your years!

EDWARD STIEGLITZ

DO THINGS WITH
**SO MUCH**
**JOY**
THAT YOU FORGET
THERE WERE
OTHER WAYS

SOMETIMES
IT JUST FEELS
REALLY, REALLY
WONDERFUL
TO BE ALIVE.

DOUGLAS COUPLAND

I'M CHOOSING HAPPINESS
OVER SUFFERING.
I'M MAKING SPACE
FOR THE UNKNOWN FUTURE
TO FILL UP MY LIFE
WITH YET-TO-COME
SURPRISES.

ELIZABETH GILBERT

Stop being afraid
of what could go wrong
and start being excited
about what could go
— right. —

TONY ROBBINS

# IT'S THE LITTLE THINGS

EVERYONE WANTS TO LIVE ON
TOP OF THE MOUNTAIN, BUT
ALL THE HAPPINESS AND
GROWTH OCCURS WHILE
YOU'RE CLIMBING IT.

ANDY ROONEY

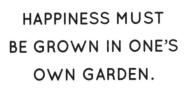

HAPPINESS MUST
BE GROWN IN ONE'S
OWN GARDEN.

MARY ENGELBREIT

FIND WHAT
MAKES YOU
HAPPY AND DO
MORE OF IT.
LOTS MORE.

THE ONLY JOY
IN THE WORLD
IS TO BEGIN.

CESARE PAVESE

BUT WHAT IS
HAPPINESS EXCEPT
THE SIMPLE HARMONY
BETWEEN A MAN AND
THE LIFE HE LEADS?

ALBERT CAMUS

Happiness is not
a state to arrive at,
but a manner
of travelling.

**Margaret
Lee Runbeck**

HAPPY MIND,
# HAPPY LIFE

VERY LITTLE IS NEEDED TO
MAKE A HAPPY LIFE; IT IS
ALL WITHIN YOURSELF, IN
YOUR WAY OF THINKING.

MARCUS AURELIUS

DOING WHAT YOU
LOVE IS FREEDOM.
*Loving*
WHAT YOU DO
IS HAPPINESS.

LANA DEL REY

# THROW
# JOY LIKE
# CONFETTI

*If you spend your whole life waiting for the storm, you'll never — enjoy the sunshine. —*

MORRIS WEST

IF YOU CAN DO
WHAT YOU DO BEST
AND BE HAPPY,
YOU ARE FURTHER
ALONG IN LIFE
THAN MOST PEOPLE.

LEONARDO DiCAPRIO

A FLOWER
BLOSSOMS FOR
ITS OWN JOY.

OSCAR WILDE

LEARN TO SEE
THE THINGS
THAT YOU MISS
EVERY DAY,
AND FIND WHOLE
NEW WORLDS
OF GRATITUDE

I'M A VERY POSITIVE THINKER,
AND I THINK THAT IS WHAT
HELPS ME THE MOST IN
DIFFICULT MOMENTS.

ROGER FEDERER

THE SECRETS
OF HAPPINESS
LIE IN OUR
CAPACITY TO

*expand*

OUR HEART.

AMIT RAY

MAKING OTHER
PEOPLE HAPPY
WILL MAKE
YOU HAPPY

THE FORMULA OF
HAPPINESS AND SUCCESS
IS JUST BEING
ACTUALLY YOURSELF,
IN THE MOST VIVID
POSSIBLE WAY YOU CAN.

MERYL STREEP

HAPPINESS
DOES NOT COME
FROM WITHOUT,
IT COMES FROM
WITHIN.

HELEN KELLER

*In order to carry*

*a positive action,*

*we must develop*

*here a*

*— positive vision. —*

DALAI LAMA

DECIDE
EVERY MORNING
THAT TODAY IS
A GOOD DAY

I MAKE POSITIVE

*choices*

SO I CAN
BE HAPPY.

HAYLEY WILLIAMS

Let a joy keep you.
Reach out your
hands and
— *take it* —
when it runs by.

CARL SANDBURG

HAPPY
# LOOKS GOOD
ON YOU

# FOLLOW
# YOUR BLISS.

JOSEPH CAMPBELL

THE FOOLISH MAN
SEEKS HAPPINESS
IN THE DISTANCE.
THE WISE GROWS IT
UNDER HIS FEET.

JAMES OPPENHEIM

To succeed in life,
you need three things:

a

— *wishbone* —

a

— *backbone* —

and a

— *funny bone.* —

REBA McENTIRE

DATE:
# TODAY.
TO DO:
# BE HAPPY!

HAPPINESS IS A RISK.
IF YOU'RE NOT
A LITTLE SCARED,
THEN YOU'RE NOT
DOING IT RIGHT.

SARAH ADDISON ALLEN

WE'RE ALL GOLDEN
SUNFLOWERS INSIDE.

ALLEN GINSBERG

SOMETIMES A SMILE IS ALL THAT STANDS BETWEEN YOU AND FEELING AWESOME

BE HAPPY,
AND A REASON
WILL COME ALONG.

ROBERT BRAULT

HAPPINESS IS NOT A GOAL...
IT'S A BY-PRODUCT OF
A LIFE WELL LIVED.

ELEANOR ROOSEVELT

The more you praise
and celebrate your life,
the more there is in
life to celebrate.

**Oprah Winfrey**

HOW YOU WISH
TO BE HAPPY IS
# ENTIRELY
DOWN TO YOU

IT IS NOT HOW MUCH WE HAVE,
BUT HOW MUCH WE ENJOY,
THAT MAKES HAPPINESS.

CHARLES SPURGEON

HAPPINESS DOESN'T
RESULT FROM
WHAT WE GET,
BUT FROM

*what we give.*

BEN CARSON

YOU
AND THIS
DAY HAVE
SO MUCH
POTENTIAL

There are so many

— great things —

in life:
why dwell on
negativity?

ZENDAYA

HAPPINESS IS NOT
A POSSESSION TO
BE PRIZED, IT IS A
QUALITY OF THOUGHT,
A STATE OF MIND.

DAPHNE DU MAURIER

YOU HAVE
TO BE WILLING
TO GET HAPPY
ABOUT NOTHING.

ANDY WARHOL

HAPPINESS,
LIKE A GOOD
PIECE OF CAKE,
SHOULD BE
SEIZED WITHOUT
DELAY

THE POWER OF
FINDING BEAUTY
IN THE HUMBLEST THINGS
MAKES HOME HAPPY
AND LIFE LOVELY.

LOUISA MAY ALCOTT

A MAN
WHO SUFFERS
OR STRESSES
BEFORE IT IS

*necessary,*

SUFFERS MORE
THAN IS
NECESSARY.

SENECA

WHEN YOU
CAN'T SEE
THE SUNSHINE,
BE THE
SUNSHINE

YOU CAN'T BE AFRAID
OF WHAT PEOPLE ARE
GOING TO SAY,
BECAUSE YOU'RE
NEVER GOING TO MAKE
EVERYONE HAPPY.

SELENA GOMEZ

LEARN TO LET GO.
THAT IS THE KEY
TO HAPPINESS.

BUDDHIST PROVERB

*The world is so full*
*of a number of things,*
*I'm sure we should*
*all be as*
*— happy as kings. —*

ROBERT LOUIS STEVENSON

LIVE SIMPLY.
GIVE MORE.
EXPECT LESS.

FOR EVERY MINUTE
YOU ARE ANGRY,
YOU LOSE

*sixty seconds*

OF HAPPINESS.

RALPH WALDO EMERSON

*Happy people are*

*— beautiful. —*

*They become
like a mirror
and they reflect
that happiness.*

DREW BARRYMORE

SIT IN
THE SUN AND
COUNT EVERY
**BEAUTIFUL**
THING YOU
CAN SEE

IF YOU WANT
TO FIND HAPPINESS,
FIND GRATITUDE.

STEVE MARABOLI

LET US BE GRATEFUL
TO THE PEOPLE WHO MAKE
US HAPPY; THEY ARE THE
CHARMING GARDENERS WHO
MAKE OUR SOULS BLOSSOM.

MARCEL PROUST

People don't
notice whether it's
— winter or summer —
when they're
happy.

ANTON CHEKHOV

# SMILE, AND WATCH AS THINGS WORK OUT

BE HAPPY FOR THIS MOMENT.
THIS MOMENT IS YOUR LIFE.

OMAR KHAYYÁM

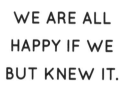

WE ARE ALL
HAPPY IF WE
BUT KNEW IT.

FYODOR DOSTOYEVSKY

If you're interested in finding out more about our books, find us on Facebook at Summersdale Publishers and follow us on Twitter at @Summersdale.

www.summersdale.com

Image credits